YOUR HARVEST IS COME

How to Give Birth to a
Three-Fold Miracle Harvest
in the Spiritual, Physical and Financial
Areas of Your Life

YOUR HARVEST IS COME

How to Give Birth to a
Three-Fold Miracle Harvest
in the Spiritual, Physical and Financial
Areas of Your Life

By
Rod Parsley

RESULTS
PUBLISHING

ISBN: 1-880244-49-7
Copyright © 1999 by Rod Parsley.

Published by:
Results Publishing
Box 32903
Columbus, Ohio 43232-0903 USA

CONTENTS

Introduction

A Three-Fold Miracle Harvest

Giving birth is never easy.

I'll never forget the thirty-six hours of labor my wife, Joni, went through to give birth to our oldest child, Ashton Blaire.

When relaying this story I always jokingly tell how hard it was for me walking the hallways of the hospital waiting for Joni to dilate enough. But obviously, she had the most difficult part.

For nine months we began to prepare mentally for the new addition to our family. We would read every book we could get on parenting.

Physically, Joni's body began to change in order to prepare for the process of giving birth. Spiritually, both of us began to pray and believe God that we would raise our child in the nurture and admonition of the Lord. The end result, or our harvest, was our beautiful daughter, Ashton!

In the spiritual realm, as you conceive the Word of God and begin to prepare for your harvest, the same thing begins to happen. You begin to get that nine month spiritual waddle. Why? You are about to give birth to something.

However, with the joy of giving birth to your miracle harvest come the labor pains, and it is at that point you are about to see a miracle.

While you anticipate your miracle harvest, the seed of the Word begins to grow inside of you. When you are walking around believing, fasting and praying for your healing, deliverance, financial breakthrough or the salvation of a lost loved one, a lot of times it sounds like a natural delivery room. At times, it may also feel as though you may be about to die and you can't push your miracle on through. But somehow, when you start to see the head of your miracle crowning, and the doctor stands up and tells you, "It's coming . . . it's coming . . . I can see it. Your miracle's coming," you receive fresh strength. Push a little harder.

Give a push of praise. Give a push of shout. Give an offering. Dance a dance. Do something to give birth to your miracle harvest. Push until something begins to happen.

Maybe you are wondering why you've been feeling so strange, why you've been hurting so bad. You're just about to give birth to a miracle. Your miracle is coming.

Today, multiplied thousands of Christians are pregnant with a dream, a desire, a hope or an aspiration. Some have been carrying their miracle for years while others have only been standing in faith a few weeks, but both are beginning to feel the labor pains of birth.

God is looking to give birth to a revolutionary movement, and it's time for you to enlist. It's time for you to take up your weapon. It's time for you to invade the corridors of the doomed and the damned, the poverty stricken and the physically stricken. It's time to thrust in the sickle and reap, for the harvest has truly come.

Jesus spoke of this prophetic hour to His disciples in John 4:35 when He said, "Say not ye, there are yet four months, and then cometh harvest? Behold I say unto you, lift up your eyes, and look on the fields; for they are white already to harvest."

Now is the time for your harvest!

In this book, I believe God has given me a very specific word for you. In it you will learn how to:

- Give birth to a three-fold miracle: spiritually, physically and financially.
- Understand how you can take an impartation of faith passed down from generation to generation.
- Reap your miracle harvest.

Maybe you are in the winter of your life; money is scarce and friends are few.

Perhaps you are feeling like a one man army as you cry yourself to sleep one more night, believing for your deliverance.

Possibly, like a woman who has carried her unborn child for nine months, the labor pains are beginning. May I remind you that it is at that moment you are about to give birth to your breakthrough. And, regardless of what the future holds, I believe that right now it is your time. . .

It is your time to give birth in the physical realm to that healing you have needed for so long.

It is time to give birth to your lost child, parent, neighbor or friend.

It is time for you to stand in the face of financial wreck and ruin and declare, "Enough is enough!"

3

Every miracle you have ever received up to this point is but a prelude to what you are about to experience.

Turn the page . . . it is time . . . for *Your Harvest is Come!*

*When the Lord turned again the captivity of Zion,
we were like them that dream (Psalm 126:1).*

One

A Dream Come True

Walking, running, leaping, crawling and any other way they could manage to stream out of the land of their captivity, the slaves set out for their long journey across the Middle Eastern desert toward the Promised Land.

For over 400 years they had served their taskmasters by the sweat of their brow and the hard labor bestowed upon them. With their faces weather beaten and their backs bearing the marks of slavery, they now raised their hands toward Yahweh.

They thought this day would never come.

Yes, some of them lived and died as slaves but they had a promise. As though the present had latched hold of the future, they could almost hear the words of the Hebrew writer echo in their ears:

> These all died in faith, not having received the promises, but having seen them afar off, and were persuaded of them, and embraced them, and confessed that they were strangers and pilgrims on the earth. For they that say such things declare plainly that they seek a country (Hebrews 11:13,14).

But it was today, and those Israelites who were alive

7

this day were singing a psalm of rejoicing:

> It seemed like a dream, too good to be true, when God returned Zion's exiles. We laughed, we sang, we couldn't believe our good fortune. We were the talk of the nations—"God was wonderful to them!" God *was* wonderful to us; we are one happy people.
>
> And now, God, do it again—bring rains to our drought-stricken lives so those who planted their crops in despair will shout hurrahs at the harvest, so those who went off with heavy hearts will come home laughing, with armloads of blessing (Psalm 126:1-4, The Message Bible).

Satan's Last Stand

Israel certainly had a reason to rejoice. They had served their Egyptian taskmasters for hundreds of years, but this particular year was their year of Jubilee. This was their year of new beginnings; their year of liberation; their year of freedom; their dream year.

But right before they left the bondage of their adversaries the devil played "Let's make a deal." Three times Pharoah tried to bargain with Moses to keep the feet of the children of Israel fettered and their hands in chains. He wanted to shackle them to a slave mentality.

First, Pharaoh told them to stay and sacrifice in the land of Egypt because he knew the Egyptians could not stand to watch them do so:

And Pharaoh called for Moses and for Aaron, and said, Go ye, sacrifice to your God in the land (Exodus 8:25).

Secondly, Pharaoh tempted them and said, "You may go but leave your children" (10:11). Satan has always been after the righteous seed because it is the righteous seed who will deliver lost and hurting humanity.

Lastly, Pharaoh told Moses that he and the children of Israel could go only if they left their cattle and flocks, for he knew if they did so they would have nothing to sacrifice unto God (10:24).

I have preached this truth so many times over the years: the last thing that Satan attempts to steal or cause you to compromise on is your money. Why? Because without it you cannot buy the necessary things you need to live, you cannot provide for your family and you cannot finance the Gospel and bring in the end time harvest of souls.

This end time hour is significant because it directly parallels the time when the children of Israel came out of Egyptian bondage. Acts 3:19-21 says:

Repent ye therefore, and be converted, that your sins may be blotted out, when the times of refreshing shall come from the presence of the Lord; And he shall send Jesus Christ, which before was preached unto you:

Whom the heaven must receive until the times of

restitution of all things, which God hath spoken by the mouth of all his holy prophets since the world began.

This is the hour when everything the Lord has promised since the fall of man in the Garden of Eden and everything the devil has stolen since the beginning of time will be restored!

An Institutionalized Truth

Throughout the Charismatic movement, we have seen several great revivals. We have seen a great revival of the Word of Faith movement. Throughout this revival, people diligently confessed the Word of God and believed they received when they prayed. This generation saw great miracles transpire in their lives as they stood on the truths of God's Word.

We have seen a great wave of a healing revival. Multiplied thousands of people were healed and delivered under great ministries like Kathryn Kuhlman, Oral Roberts, A.A. Allen and many others.

Today, we are seeing a great revival of salvation. Tens of thousands of people are giving their lives to God every day. We are truly reaping a great harvest of souls.

But of all the great revivals of the Spirit of God there is one area in which the body of Christ has not experienced a great outpouring and that is in the area of finances.

Satan's goal is to keep you in bondage to poverty. The Bible plainly states, "Money answereth all things" (Ecclesiastes 10:19).

One day as I was meditating on this I asked the Lord, "Why has the body of Christ as a whole not seen a great harvest in finances? We have seen a trickle here and a trickle there but we have not experienced the great outpouring which was prophesied by the prophet Malachi when he said,

> Bring ye all the tithes into the storehouse, that there may be meat in mine house, and prove me now herewith, saith the Lord of hosts, if I will not open you the windows of heaven, and pour you out a blessing, that there shall not be room enough to receive it (3:10).

It was at that point that the Lord began unveil this profound truth to me:

> One generation receives a revelation from the Lord about a particular truth, such as healing, confession, salvation (those things which I named previously.) The next generation begins to walk in that truth and then begins to experience the reality of God's spoken Word.

> However, by the third generation that great holy revelation begins to become institutionalized, and it becomes stripped of its power by those who want to mix it with their own man-made doctrine. Then by the next generation that truth is all but dead.

Let me just interject this here. God will not be mixed with anything or anyone. He will not be mixed with our unbelief, doubt or religious traditions. Nothing changes who God is . . . He is God all by Himself!

As this revelation began to unfold in my spirit, it was as if a light switch was turned on. It was at that point the Lord revealed to me the passage in James 5:1-3:

> Go to now, ye rich men, weep and howl for your miseries that shall come upon you. Your riches are corrupted, and your garments are moth-eaten.

> Your gold and silver is cankered; and the rust of them shall be a witness against you, and shall eat your flesh as it were fire. Ye have heaped treasure together for the last days.

God continued to reveal to me that if He had given this revelation on finances before the time in which you and I are living, it would have eventually burned out like a smoldering fire.

This reminds me of the Israelites I mentioned at the beginning of this chapter. Even though Moses had made the proclamation of freedom to the children of Israel who were released from Egyptian bondage, they had joy in the declared Word of the Lord only for the moment. They would never enter into the Promised Land! This generation never received the revelation that God brought them out of slavery in order to take them into blessing!

All of the adult children would die without inheriting the promise! What a staggering thought! Why, you may ask? Because they did not act upon the Word of God declared unto them! They had a slave mentality!

Though they had been delivered from Egyptian bondage, spiritually their feet were still fettered and their hands were still in chains. They were used to living from day-to-day with what the Egyptians gave them; therefore, when they went into the wilderness they were satisfied living only on manna and quail and wearing shoes that never wore out!

But God had made a promise and He had already made the provision to possess the Promised Land. In His heart He knew there would be a people who would not settle for a life of low living, sight walking and tame vision. He saw through the telescope of eternity a remnant—a people within a nation, a man within a family, a church within a church—who would take Him at his Word.

The Last Great Harvest

You and I are living in a time when the reaper is going to overtake the sower. You and I are living in an hour where we are going to give birth to a three-fold harvest in the spiritual, physical and financial areas of our lives.

In this final hour we are seeing a restitution of all things. Just as with Israel when there was not one feeble one among them, so it will be with this final generation. As it was when the Israelites took their righteous seed, or harvest of souls, with them, I believe we will continue to see a great influx of the lost into the kingdom of God.

Just as it was when the children of Israel were laden with the wealth of Egypt insomuch that they could barely carry it off, so I believe it will be with us. We are going to experience a three-fold harvest . . . a harvest in every area of our lives.

It's Raining Upstream

You and I are like the Israelites when they left Egyptian bondage. We are like those who dreamed a dream. We are like calves loosed from the stall. We are living in a dream world where the free favors of God profusely abound.

You may be in the valley, but it's raining upstream. The tributaries are already full and overflowing. There's something coming down out of the mountain, cascading into the valley of your human experience. There's a flood on the way!

You may be dry and parched right now, but it's raining upstream. You may not have a dollar to change today, but it's raining upstream. Your kids may be lost today, but it's raining upstream. You may not see signs of harvest in any area of your life, but it's raining upstream.

And in this hour, Jehovah God promised through the prophet Joel, "Be glad then, ye children of Zion, and rejoice in the Lord your God: for he hath given you the former rain moderately, and he will cause to come down for you the rain, the former rain, and the latter rain in the first month.

And the floors shall be full of wheat, and the fats shall overflow with wine and oil. And I will restore to you the years that the locust hath eaten, the cankerworm, and the caterpillar, and the palmerworm, my great army which I sent among you" (Joel 2:23-25).

At the foundation of the church at this moment, there is a standard shift, like a fault line moving, separating. Something is happening. There is a polarization going on. The hot seem to be getting hotter while the cold seem to be getting colder.

There are those who are coming out of seeming obscurity, like John the Baptist and Abraham. They are rich, but have the testimony that no man made them rich . . . rich in spiritual power . . . rich in anointing . . . rich in authority.

The body of Christ is preparing for this three-fold harvest and in doing so they are preparing for change. When change comes, those who are not prepared will be crushed by it. Those who are prepared will be as those who, on a surfboard, find the tunnel of the wave and are propelled into a position that before they never dreamed possible.

We must learn to adjust our sails. We are at what Andy Grove, CEO and Founder of the Intel Corporation calls a "strategic inflection point"—a point where a decision between two alternatives must be made. We have hit a wall, and we must go one way or the other.

Every fresh new golden era of human history has always been preceded by the devotion and righteous passion of one or more individuals. It only takes a few who know their God to do exploits and receive this end time three-fold harvest . . . and God always has a remnant.

In these last days the Lord is opening doors around the world, in your city, your neighborhood and your family. He is swinging wide the door of financial freedom and physical healing. Why? Because it is harvest time.

In the next chapter I'm going to show you that no longer are you going to have to wait for your three-fold harvest. No longer do you have to die without your promise because you harvest is already on the way!

Behold, the days come, saith the LORD, that the plowman shall overtake the reaper, and the treader of grapes him that soweth seed; and the mountains shall drop sweet wine, and all the hills shall melt (Amos 9:13).

Two

Preparing for Your Harvest

A few years ago I went fishing with a close friend of mine out on the Gulf of Mexico, just off the Florida coastline. I could hardly wait to go. I had been preaching several nights on the road, away from my family and my church, and I was looking forward to this much needed rest.

When we first cast our lines I was so excited I couldn't wait for the first bite. Hours later, red as a lobster and with no sign of any fish anywhere, I was ready to call it quits when my friend pulled the throttle on the boat and began racing across the water.

Startled and almost knocked off my feet, I asked him what he was doing and where he was going. He said, "Do you see that pile of wood floating over there? That's where I'm headed."

Needless to say, I was beginning to think the sun had gotten the best of him. I said, "We haven't caught anything yet and those old boards don't look good enough to eat!"

He responded, "There are fish under those planks."

Once we stopped we began casting our lines into the water, and in what seemed like only a few seconds the fish began to bite. One right after the other, we were reeling in those fish.

We were pulling them in so quickly we could barely get them off of our lines. One particular instance I was reeling in a catch when another big fish jumped out of the water and snatched my fish right off my line!

In these last days, I believe that is what it is going to be like in the body of Christ and for you. You are going to receive your three-fold harvest all at once, so drastically and unexpectedly, that you won't even be able to keep up with how God is going to bless you!

The Gospel of Mark says it this way,

So is the kingdom of God, as if a man should cast seed into the ground; And should sleep, and rise night and day, and the seed should spring and grow up, he knoweth not how. For the earth bringeth forth fruit of herself; first the blade, then the ear, after that the full corn in the ear. But when the fruit is brought forth, immediately he putteth in the sickle, because the harvest is come (4:26-29).

The harvest cannot wait. It is the shortest period of time in the reproductive growth of your seed. You can leave your seed in your barn for years, plant it and it will still bring forth a harvest when you plant it.

It is harvest time not only for souls, but also for everything else in your life. We are in the season of harvest. When the grain fields turn golden brown, the harvest cannot sit in the fields for long before being reaped.

Another friend of mine harvests grain. When it is

planting season, there is a space of time when the ground is conducive to receive the seed. When it is growing season, there is a span of time when the seed is receiving its nutrients from the sun and rain. But when it is harvest time, he cannot wait to harvest. My friend will stay out on his combine all night to get his crops in. Why? Because harvest is the shortest season there is, and if he waits too long, then his crops will die in the field.

So many have crops that have rotted in the field. We have been blaming God for not answering our prayer when, in reality, He gave seed to the sower, the sower sowed the seed and God gave the increase.

The seed will do what it is supposed to do; it is the nature of a seed to reproduce. It is not our responsibility to know how the seed grows. The seed and the soil will do what they are supposed to do. God will do His part because it is God who giveth the increase.

You have yet to pray a prayer that He did not answer. Every seed that you have ever sown has produced a harvest. Because you have not actively known how to harvest your seed it ruined in the field. He heard your prayer and He answered that prayer. He multiplied your seed sown.

Genesis 8:22 says, "While the earth remaineth, seedtime and harvest [planting time and reaping time], and cold and heat, and summer and winter, and day and night shall not cease." God made no mention of what goes on between seedtime and harvest.

The closer we get to the soon and imminent return of Jesus Christ of Nazareth the shorter time will become.

Time is going to shrink.

Take, for instance, when someone breaks an arm or a leg. I know when I broke my arm as a boy that it took nearly eight weeks for it to mend. When it did mend, though, and the doctor took the cast off, atrophy had set in. It was smaller than my other arm because it had been in the same position all that time. The muscle had begun to give way.

When this end time harvest comes there will be no space of time between your seed sown and when you reap your harvest. Just as when my broken arm was restored, your harvest will be restored to new as instantly as the anointing of God can penetrate it!

Just as the treader of grapes tramples grapes under his feet when he hasn't sown any seed yet, as quickly as your seed hits the ground, you are going to harvest it.

God said He would do a quick work in these last days. The harvest is coming quickly. We don't have time to play around in the playpen of mediocrity.

We need to start expecting a return. We need to begin to understand God's Word concerning harvesting. We are the harvest generation.

Today is the Day
On May 15, 1948 the gavel came down in the halls of the United Nations, and Israel—who had been scattered since the dispersal in 70 A.D. at the destruction of the temple by Titus in the city of Jerusalem—once again became a nation. It was the year of Jubilee.

In that year every slave was set free. Every debt was canceled. But most importantly everything went back to God—their houses, their land, their cattle, their sheep, their minds—everything!

When Jesus walked, the earth under the anointing of the Holy Spirit, He walked into the synagogue in Nazareth and there He was handed the book of the prophet Isaiah and began to read:

> The Spirit of the Lord God is upon me; because the Lord hath anointed me to preach good tidings unto the meek; he hath sent me to bind up the brokenhearted, to proclaim liberty to the captives, and the opening of the prison to them that are bound; to proclaim the acceptable year of the LORD, and the day of vengeance of our God; to comfort all that mourn;

> To appoint unto them that mourn in Zion, to give unto them beauty for ashes, the oil of joy for mourning, the garment of praise for the spirit of heaviness; that they might be called trees of righteousness, the planting of the Lord, that he might be glorified (Isaiah 61:1-3).

The acceptable year of the Lord translated means the year when the free favors of God profusely abound. The Message Bible says it this way: *The year when God chooses to act!* (Luke 4:19).

In essence, I believe God was saying, "You have prayed long enough. You have fasted long enough. Now

I am about to take control of your situation. I am about to destroy every oppressor. I am about to loose every bondage in your life."

It was at that point that Jesus closed the book. Why? Because He had just given us a revelation of who He was. He went over to the chair reserved for the High Priest and sat down in it. Then He announced, "This day is this scripture fulfilled in your ears" (Luke 4:21).

It is time to stop looking at a calendar. When is Jubilee? I have said it so many times: It is the day that you receive a revelation of who Jesus is.

Make Preparation—Your Harvest is Here!

As I stated earlier, we must be prepared to reap the bountiful harvest to come like there's no tomorrow, because the harvest is the shortest season.

Time is short! There isn't a moment to waste in this dimension of the acceleration of time.

We were anointed for this time. The word "anoint" means to smear on, rub in, immerse or paint. You and I have been painted with the fragrance which attracts the blessing and free favors of God. You may not realize it, but this is your year of favor, and it is time for you to receive your harvest!

During the Gulf War the Allied Forces used stealth bombers which were undetectable to enemy radar. One of them was equipped with a laser. That laser would lock in on a target and shoot a beam of light toward it. The light would dissipate and leave behind only minute particles of light undetectable to anything but a smart bomb. The smart bomb would then follow that trace of light and hit its target with pinpoint accuracy. Just like you are painted with the anointing, that target had been painted.

God said, "I'm going to draw a target on your life. I'm going to paint you, so when you're in the darkness of your midnight hour my blessing can find you." That's why Malachi said the blessings of God will overtake you.

When you were born, you weren't born with a rattle in your hand; you were born with a sickle. You are a reaper in this revolutionary, end time remnant army . . . and God saved the best for last. We are going to reap what John Wesley, Martin Luther, Howard Carter and Dr. Sumrall sowed. Get into the fields! They are white already to harvest (John 4:35)!

How do you reap your harvest? Number one, you send forth your angels according to Hebrews 1:14. They are just waiting to be released by the words of your mouth to go and get what you need. There are things such as healing, salvation and deliverance that you have sown for over the years but have yet to reap.

Number two, you need to prophesy your harvest in. Revelation 19:10 says, "The testimony of Jesus is the spirit of prophecy." It was spoken words that brought Jesus out of that tomb. David said you will not suffer me to see death neither will thou leave my soul in hell (Psalm 16:10).

He told the disciples before they were His disciples, "Come, and I will make you fishers of men." God is intent on making you into that which He wants you to be, and He wants to make you the righteousness of God in Christ Jesus.

His Word declares, "Yet, have I not seen the righteous forsaken, nor His seed begging for bread" (Psalm 37:25). In fact, your Bible said God would supply seed for the sowing and bread for the eating (Isaiah 55:10).

God does not intend for His church to have a begging mentality, a missionary barrel mentality or a barely getting by mentality. He doesn't want us to walk around wishing we could find the ends, much less make them meet mentality.

There is a revelation that has come to the body of Christ which is leading us from the back of the bus and moving us into the forefront where we are going to take control. It is the revelation that there is a three-fold harvest — spiritually, physically and financially — for all who will learn to operate in the truths of faith that I am going to share with you in the upcoming chapters.

3 John 2 says, "Beloved, I pray that you may prosper in every way and that [your body] may keep well, even as [I know] your soul keeps well and prospers" (Amplified).

How long will we continue to believe Scriptures like this are for someone else?

How long will we continue to rejoice at someone else's miracle?

How long until we turn our hands heavenward and begin to take God at His Word and, in faith believing, receive it as our own? Hebrews 11:1 declares, "Now faith is the assurance (the confirmation, the title deed) of the things [we] hope for, being the proof of things [we] do not see and the conviction of their reality [faith perceiving as real fact what is not revealed to the senses" (Amplified).

In these last two chapters we have learned how God is pouring out His Spirit in these last days to cause us to receive a three-fold miracle harvest. Now it is time to act on it individually for ourselves and our own household!

Faith will take the promise of your future,
which was given in your past,
and make your harvest manifest in your present.

Three

A Seed of Faith

One day, a fellow was in the park reading his Bible when an atheist passed by and asked him, "Why are you reading that book? It's full of contradictions." This believer calmly slid the Bible across the picnic table to the atheist and said, "Is that right? Open it up and show me one."

The Bible is the infallible, inerrant Word of the living God. The Bible is tried and tested, and though heaven and earth rock and reel like a drunken man, under the pressure of the hour, the Word of God will remain forever!

In order to stand in the midnight of your situation, you must have faith in the unchanging Word of God.

Psalm 138:2 says, "For thou hast magnified thy word above all thy name."

Isaiah 55:10,11 proclaims, "For as the rain cometh down, and the snow from heaven, and returneth not thither, but watereth the earth, and maketh it bring forth and bud, that it may give seed to the sower, and bread to the eater: So shall my word be that goeth forth out of my mouth: it shall not return unto me void, but it shall accomplish that which I please, and it shall prosper *in the thing* whereto I sent it."

Great men and women of faith have clung to the Word of God in their dying hour as their source of hope and comfort.

In the midnight hour of the aching, desperate soul, the Bible has been like a well springing up to life. The miracle harvest they sought for days, months and maybe even years came from heaven and invaded their life.

For instance, it was midnight when Samson possessed the gates of the city. It was midnight when, from the jail cell, it rang as Paul and Silas sang. It was midnight when Boaz was revealed to Ruth as her kinsman redeemer.

Midnight is the perfect time to release a shout of praise. Anyone can sing a tune on a clear day at noon, but I want a song to sing at midnight when trouble all around is closing in.

Perfect faith begins where the will of God is known. Therefore, first and foremost, you must know the will of God, through His Word, before you can stand in faith toward God.

Faith's Foundation Stone

Faith is not complicated. Faith is not some ethereal, philosophical idea floating around out there with eastern mysticism. You must begin with the building block and foundational stone of, "I know this is God's will."

Hebrews 11:1 says, "Now, faith is the substance of things hoped for and the evidence of things not seen." Faith is the favorable and confident expectation of things not perceived with the sensory mechanisms. Why?

30

Because the things you can feel, smell, taste, hear and see are subject to change."

The Gospel of Luke gives us a perfect illustration where this very question was asked of Jesus, "If it be thy will":

> And it came to pass, when he was in a certain city, behold a man full of leprosy: who seeing Jesus fell on his face, and besought him, saying, Lord, if thou wilt, thou canst make me clean (5:12).

This is the only place in the New Testament where Jesus of Nazareth was asked the question, "If you will." In response, Jesus put forth His hand and touched the leper, saying, "I will."

You will never find a place in the New Testament where Jesus said, "I won't!"

This is the riveting question in the mind of every believer when they are trying to step from the natural into the supernatural and to walk by faith but not by sight. The struggle with most Christians is not with God's ability. The greatest struggle is knowing His will for our lives. Thus, an understanding of the will of God gives you the foundational stone whereby you can stand in faith.

When reading in the Bible, "God takes pleasure in the prosperity of his servant," you need to stand upon that Word.

It is His will to heal you according to 1 Peter 2:24, so stand and declare, "By His stripes, I am healed."

Why? Because the Bible proclaims, "The just shall live by faith" (Romans 1:17).

The Apostle Peter is another wonderful example of this truth:

> And when he had sent the multitudes away, he went up into a mountain apart to pray: and when the evening was come, he was there alone. But the ship was now in the midst of the sea, tossed with waves: for the wind was contrary.
>
> And in the fourth watch of the night Jesus went unto them, walking on the sea. And when the disciples saw him walking on the sea, they were troubled, saying, It is a spirit; and they cried out for fear.
>
> But straightway Jesus spake unto them, saying, Be of good cheer; it is I; be not afraid. And Peter answered him and said, Lord, if it be thou, bid me come unto thee on the water. And he said, Come. And when Peter was come down out of the ship, he walked on the water, to go to Jesus (Matthew 14:23-29).

Every time you determine to stand upon the Word of God, you will begin to get a vision of something painted on the inside of you that may not make sense in the natural realm. No one may seem to understand you. In fact, at times you may not even understand yourself. Like Peter, everyone may be telling you that you can't get out of the boat and walk on water.

However, I believe if you were to ask Peter about what happened he would have turned around and told you, "I didn't walk on the water. Jesus said to me, 'Come.' When He said that, His Word, like an invisible plank, was laid across the top of the water. I didn't walk on the water; I walked upon His Word!"

Walking on water is impossible, but walking on the Word is absolutely possible. The Bible declares, "And Jesus looking upon them saith, With men it is impossible, but not with God: for with God all things are possible" (Mark 10:27).

A couple in our church latched onto the Word of the Lord in faith when they were handed a baby that had just a brain stem but no brain. His head was swollen as big as his shoulders.

When the doctors handed them their baby, they didn't give him any hope of living, much less of having any semblance of a normal life. But they had faith in the Word of God and His ability to give them their harvest.

They believed it isn't any harder for God to create a brain outside the womb, than it is for God to create a brain inside the womb. Today, their son has a fully developed brain. They received their miracle harvest.

Your Harvest Is "Yes" and "Amen"

What each of us in the body of Christ needs to understand is that whenever we ask God anything, His promises are "yes" and "amen" to those who believe.

Therefore, if you can claim one of God's promises, and lay hold of it with pit-bull faith . . . then you can stare the devil down and say, "You can't make me nervous. I know it's God's will. You can't tempt me and say, 'Well, God would never want that.' I know, that I know, that I know it is God's will!"

If you can grab ahold of the promise and then know that it's His will, then you can understand that to every promise, His answer is, "Yes!" Every promise in the Bible, His answer is, "I will!" Every promise is "So be it," "Amen, to them who believe."

Will you heal me? Jesus answers, "I will." Will you bless me? Again He declares, "I will." Will you save my children? Jesus hails a resounding, "Yes!"

However, you can't operate with blind faith. You have to have a word. You have to receive, in the depths of your spirit, a Word from the Lord. Then you latch hold of a promise such as, Me and my house, we shall be saved (Acts 16:31), and stand in faith believing until that seed of the Word becomes a full grown harvest of salvation! There's the promise!

An Immediate Harvest
Let's look again at the man with the leprosy who cried out to Jesus, "Lord, if thou wilt, thou canst make me clean" (Luke 5:12).

How long did it take Jesus to heal the man with leprosy? The Bible goes on to say,

> And immediately the leprosy departed from him. And he charged him to tell no man: but go, and shew thyself to the priest, and offer for thy cleansing, according as Moses commanded, for a testimony unto them (Luke 5:13,14).

God is sending an immediate harvest to His people in these last days. Just as with the leper above, whomever His Spirit touches will receive their three-fold harvest.

Your ability to reap your harvest is not about you. It's about God backing up His Word. Numbers 23:19 says, "God is not a man, that he should lie; neither the son of man, that he should repent: hath he said, and shall he not do it? or hath he spoken, and shall he not make it good?"

God will make good on His promises. He will pour out His abundant harvest in every area of your life!

Faith to Frame Your World

By faith, we understand the universe was framed. You can frame your world by faith.

We are taking back our spiritual, physical and financial harvests that belong to us. How can we do that? Because God doesn't change, and what He promised in His Word He will do!

What does it mean that God doesn't change? It means what He was, He is, and what He is, He will be. Because

He never changes, you and I can have faith in His faithfulness.

Moses had great faith in God's faithfulness. Why? He met God in the desert through a burning bush. He had an experience with Yahweh. Because of that Moses could respond when God said, "Go tell Pharaoh that I AM sent me."

God never demands faith beyond your experience with Him. He lays your life out with a series of instances where you must apply faith to make it through. He then proves Himself faithful in those areas so He can take you to another level.

That's the reason 2 Thessalonians 1:3 says, "Your faith groweth exceedingly." Why? Because your revelation of Him continues to expand. He continues to prove Himself faithful to His Word, so that you realize He said it, and He did it.

If you and I are going to have faith, we need to have a revelation of Jesus—we need to know who is talking to us. After we know this, we must know what He said. After we know what He said, then we must know, "Does He have a track record?" Is He faithful to what He said?

However, once you get to know Jesus and understand who He is, you then begin to have faith in His Word. After you have walked with Him you will discover He is Jehovah Raphe, the God that healeth you.

Then when the doctor looks at you and tells you, "You have cancer and have to die and not live," you can say, "Wait a minute. I have a higher authority. I hear your word, Doctor, but I have another word drowning you out. I'm sorry, the frequency's breaking up! I can't hear you. I have another message coming in, and it declares, 'By His stripes, I am healed.'"

Then you can stand on that word when there isn't anything else to stand on. You can hope against hope, and you can believe beyond belief. You can stand steadfast and say, "God declared it. He will establish it; and though heaven and earth shall pass away, His Word shall remain."

When you stand on God's Word, people may laugh at you. When a second opinion is worse than the first, still cling to that Word. Job 22:28 says, "Thou shalt also decree a thing, and it shall be established unto thee."

I've Been There Before

Imagine for a moment you are an Israelite. Maybe you have just been freed from Egyptian bondage, but now you are between a rock and a hard place. You are up against the Red Sea, with Pi-hahiroth and Migdol on one side of you, Baal-zephon behind you and the pursuing Egyptian army staring you in the face. There is nothing stretched out before you, but the sea, and there you stand. Hearing the clanking and the clattering of your adverary's chariots, you do not tuck tail and run.

When God says, "Go," you start wading out into the sea water as sea weed wraps around your legs, believing in the natural you are surely going to die. You thought you would never make it to the other side, but instead would be swallowed up by the billowing waves of defeat. But, now you stand, and you keep on walking.

Now, you have water up around your knees. Everybody is getting nervous. Everybody is saying, "Aren't you going to turn around?" But your faith goes back to when you were baking bricks. You can almost feel the lash of Pharaoh's whip upon your back. However, your mind echoes the words of Yahweh, "I shall bring you out with a strong right arm." Now your hope is about to become faith!

Maybe you are in dire financial need. You have balanced your checking account. You have checked your calculator, torn up the ribbon and thrown it away. You have added up your money, but no matter how you look at it, it is still a bad report when you get to the bottom line.

Possibly you have been believing for your teenager to come out of the situation they're in. Yet, Friday night when they came home in a drunken stupor, you began to wonder if things were ever going to change.

Everywhere you turn you recieve a bad report. And, to make matters, worse, it isn't even Sunday morning where the preacher is preaching a power-packed message, the organ is playing, the choir is singing and thousands of people are adding their faith to yours. It's just you now.

It's the middle of the week, and trouble all around is closing in. There's no light anywhere. The darkness of your human experience beats upon you. You feel as if there's no way you're going to make it.

Somehow, though, you stand there in the middle of that darkness, and raise your hands. You lift a voice that no one can hear but you and begin to speak Jehovah's Word.

"Thy word is a lamp unto my feet, and a light unto my path" (Psalm 119:105). You have no outward evidence, but instead you have the illumination of His Word. Jesus said it. You believe it, and it's so.

You can see the light and the illumination of that Word. There is nothing to stand on but that Word, but what else do you need? He spoke His Word, and the universe leaped into being.

He uttered His Word from the bow of a ship, His Word shot across the stormy Sea of Galilee, and Peter climbed over the boat. He wasn't walking on the water. You can't walk on water. He was walking on the Word. That's something you can walk on. The prophet Isaiah declared, "For thou hast been a strength to the poor, a strength to the needy in his distress, a refuge from the storm, a shadow from the heat, when the blast of the terrible ones is as a storm against the wall" (25:4).

God is a mighty refuge in the midst of the storms of your life. He is a strength, a strong tower and a refuge. He will never allow you to sink in the billows of trials and tribulation.

As long as you zero in on God's Word that cannot fail, the storms and the dark clouds will rise but they won't worry you. You know you'll receive your three-fold harvest. Why? You are sheltered safe within the arms of God!

With every spoken Word of faith,
like a painter taking a paintbrush
and beginning to draw an image out of nothing,
God begins to paint an image of your harvest on the
inside of you, and stamps it so indelibly upon you that
hell, itself, can't wipe it off.

Four

The Voice of Your Seed

With one word God spoke galaxies and worlds into existence. By His spoken word, He flung the stars into orbit, hung the sun and the moon, set the earth spinning on its axis and commanded the ocean not to spill a drop of water.

Genesis 1:1-3 declares, "In the beginning God created the heaven and the earth. And the earth was without form, and void; and darkness was upon the face of the deep. And the Spirit of God moved upon the face of the waters. And God said, Let there be light: and there was light."

The New Testament counterpart for this passage of Scripture says, "In the beginning was the Word, and the Word was with God, and the Word was God. And the Word was made flesh, and dwelt among us, (and we beheld his glory, the glory as of the only begotten of the Father), full of grace and truth" (John 1:1, 14).

God and His Word are synonymous. What is a word? It is a divine thought communicated.

The woman with the issue of blood is a perfect example of speaking the Word, for the Gospel of Mark records:

> And a certain woman, which had an issue of blood twelve years, and had suffered many things of many physicians, and had spent all that she had, and was nothing bettered, but rather grew worse, when she had heard of Jesus, came in the press behind, and touched his garment.
>
> For she said, If I may touch but his clothes, I shall be whole. And straightway the fountain of her blood was dried up; and she felt in her body that she was healed of that plague (Mark 5:25-29).

The Word Speaks

Jesus was on his way to minister to a high official, Jairus', daughter. This woman pressed through the crowd as they tried to beat her away. She was unclean. No one was allowed to touch her and she was not supposed to touch anyone.

But what was the first thing she did? She heard Jesus was in town. This woman had possibly heard stories of the multitudes Jesus had healed from town to town. Perhaps she heard the story of blind Bartimaeus. Maybe one of her relatives shared with her the wonderful display of compassion and deliverance toward the young child who often cast himself into the fire. Something so stirred her to the very depths of her spirit to believe this man, the carpenter's son, could heal her also.

Secondly, she spoke to herself. Do you know why? Because no one else believed her. And, as an artist would begin to paint on a canvas, her words began to paint an image of her being whole on her spirit.

Faith will cause you to talk to yourself. There are two hinges to your faith found in Romans chapter 10 and verse 10 which says, "For with the heart man believeth unto righteousness; and with the mouth confession is made unto salvation."

Third, she touched the hem of His garment. The word "touch" here is the Greek word "hepto" or to take hold of. Like Jacob wrestling with the angel at the brook at Jabbock all night, he took hold of God. This woman grabbed hold of Jesus with pit-bull faith.

Number four, she felt healing come in and sickness go out! Once she touched the border of Jesus' garment she was immediately set free! How wonderful one touch can be. Many were in the crowd that day and thronged Him. They were familiar with the outward signs of a carpenter whose face was weather beaten and whose hands were calloused. But this woman grasped hold of the King within. Human curiosity and human interest pressed at Jesus through the crowd.

The faith of this woman touched Him, and He was arrested by her belief. Flesh always presses, but faith always touches.

God will allow you to use His word, spoken up out of

a faith-filled heart, to cover your heart, like a paintbrush, with an image of your harvest. You will begin to see your spouse saved. You will begin to picture your child being healed. You will begin to feel your mind being delivered. You will start to imagine your all of your bills paid with thousands of dollars left over to help minister the Gospel.

The Word is Nigh

Remember, in previous chapters, I shared with you that faith is not an idea, faith is not a philosophy and faith is not a thought. Rather, faith is an act, spoken through your words and demonstrated by expression. It's the word of faith.

The Book of Romans declares, "But what saith it? The word is nigh thee, even in thy mouth, and in thy heart: that is, the word of faith, which we preach" (10:8).

The Gospel of Mark 11:22-24 reiterates this message when it records:

And Jesus answering saith unto them, Have faith in God. For verily I say unto you, That whosoever shall say unto this mountain, Be thou removed, and be thou cast into the sea; and shall not doubt in his heart, but shall believe that those things which he saith shall come to pass; he shall have whatsoever he saith.

Therefore I say unto you, What things soever ye desire, when ye pray, believe that ye receive them, and ye shall have them.

Second Corinthians 4:13 says it this way, "I believed, and therefore have I spoken."

Faith without works is dead. Again, I have believed, therefore have I spoken. Romans 10:14 states:

> How then shall they call on him in whom they have not believed? and how shall they believe in him of whom they have not heard? and how shall they hear without a preacher?

The process does not begin with calling, nor does it begin with believing, because faith cometh by hearing. Faith is nothing more than information in manifestation, and God never demands faith beyond your knowledge of Him. He never commanded Moses to tell Pharaoh to let the children of Israel go before He spoke to him from a burning bush. Moses had faith in the faithfulness of God.

You cannot call until you have believed, and you cannot believe until you have heard. You cannot hear without an understanding of spiritual authority, where a God-ordained, five-fold ministry gift is operating in the prophetic realm.

The five-fold ministry gift receives a word from the Lord and then communicates it to the people, because Proverb 29:18 says:

> Where there is no vision, the people perish: but he that keepeth the law, happy is he.

With the hearing of the preacher comes an impartation of faith in the spoken Word of God. Timothy experienced this when the Bible records, "When I call to remembrance the unfeigned faith that is in thee, which dwelt first in thy grandmother Lois, and thy mother Eunice; and I am persuaded that in thee also" (2 Timothy 1:5).

If you are in line with God's Word, then you have an impartation of faith in your life as well, from those whom you have submitted your life to. In my life, when I speak to great congregations of people, out of my voice comes Dr. Lester Sumrall's faith. Out of my voice, through him, comes Smith Wigglesworth's faith. Out of my voice comes Howard Carter's faith, which was imparted to Smith Wigglesworth, and on it goes.

When you understand this, then you can believe that prophetic word and then you can call upon God according to Jeremiah 33:3, "Call unto me, and I will answer thee, and shew thee great and mighty things, which thou knowest not."

Herein lies the reality of faith in submission to authority. Matthew 8:5-10 proclaims,

> And when Jesus was entered into Capernaum, there came unto him a centurion, beseeching him, and saying, Lord, my servant lieth at home sick of the palsy, grievously tormented.
>
> And Jesus saith unto him, I will come and heal him.

The centurion answered and said, Lord, I am not worthy that thou shouldest come under my roof: but speak the word only, and my servant shall be healed.

For I am a man under authority, having soldiers under me: and I say to this man, Go, and he goeth; and to another, Come, and he cometh; and to my servant, Do this, and he doeth it. When Jesus heard it, he marveled, and said to them that followed, Verily I say unto you, I have not found so great faith, no, not in Israel.

He had submitted himself to the authority of Jesus, understanding that whatever Jesus said would come to pass, because He has a proven track record.

When God created man, He gave him the same creative ability He possessed to speak things into being because He formed man in His image. Genesis 1:26-27 says, "And God said, Let us make man in our image, after our likeness: and let them have dominion over the fish of the sea, and over the fowl of the air, and over the cattle, and over all the earth, and over every creeping thing that creepeth upon the earth. So God created man in his own image, in the image of God created he him; male and female created he them."

Because we are created in the likeness of God, we can have what we say—the good as well as the bad. Proverb 18:21 proclaims, "Death and life are in the power of the tongue: and they that love it shall eat the fruit thereof."

Genesis chapter 11 illustrates how the people of the earth began to put this truth into operation.

And the whole earth was of one language, and of one speech. And it came to pass, as they journeyed from the east, that they found a plain in the land of Shinar; and they dwelt there.

And they said one to another, Go to, let us make brick, and burn them throughly. And they had brick for stone, and slime had they for morter. And they said, Go to, let us build us a city and a tower, whose top may reach unto heaven; and let us make us a name, lest we be scattered abroad upon the face of the whole earth.

And the Lord came down to see the city and the tower, which the children of men builded. And the Lord said, Behold, the people is one, and they have all one language; and this they begin to do: and now nothing will be restrained from them, which they have imagined to do. Go to, let us go down, and there confound their language, that they may not understand one another's speech (11:1-7).

The people were of one voice, speaking the same thing. They couldn't speak what they hadn't believed. They couldn't believe what they hadn't heard. And they couldn't hear unless there was a prophetic unction.

Because humanity was fashioned in the likeness of Jehovah, they began to imitate their Father and to talk just like Him. They were calling things that be not as though they were.

God's response was, in essence, to end their ability to converse with one another, otherwise, nothing would be impossible to them. However, let me make this statement: If the Lord can ever get a group of people together—a remnant will do—who begin to say the same thing according to His Word, then He can stand upon His throne and declare, "Nothing that they imagine shall be impossible to them."

If God can ever get the body of Christ to begin to say the same thing, then God can stand upon His throne and declare, Nothing that they imagine shall be impossible to them.

When you receive a Word into your spirit and say it repeatedly, you will get to the point that you believe it. Once you believe it, then you will speak it. And, when you speak it, it's not just you speaking, it is God speaking through you.

Your ability to call upon God is directly linked to your ability to believe . . . which is directly linked to your ability to hear . . . which is directly linked to your ability to operate under the spiritual authority God has placed in your life.

Once you hear and believe, then you can do something, which gives expression to the faith that's in your heart. The number one thing you can do to give expression to the faith that's in your heart is to call upon God.

Here are some examples of what you can declare:

Psalm 107:20, "He sent his word, and healed them, and delivered them from their destructions."

Proverb 18:21, "Death and life are in the power of the tongue: and they that love it shall eat the fruit thereof."

John 6:63, "It is the spirit that quickeneth; the flesh profiteth nothing: the words that I speak unto you, they are spirit, and they are life."

Acts 2:22-24, "Ye men of Israel, hear these words; Jesus of Nazareth, a man approved of God among you by miracles and wonders and signs, which God did by him in the midst of you, as ye yourselves also know:

Him, being delivered by the determinate counsel and foreknowledge of God, ye have taken, and by wicked hands have crucified and slain: Whom God hath raised up, having loosed the pains of death: because it was not possible that he should be holden of it."

2 Timothy 2:9, "Wherein I suffer trouble, as an evil doer, even unto bonds; but the word of God is not bound."

A Harvest in Winter

In Jeremiah God asked the prophet this question:

Moreover the word of the Lord came unto me, saying, Jeremiah, what seest thou? And I said, I see a rod of an almond tree. Then said the Lord unto me, Thou hast well seen: for I will hasten my word to perform it (1:11,12).

An almond tree does not bear fruit in the winter. Jeremiah saw something that was out of the realm of normalcy. He saw something beyond the natural, something supernatural. He saw the rod of an almond tree, hanging full of almonds, in the middle of the winter. And God said, "As a result, I will hasten after my Word."

Here, just outside of Columbus, in a little town called Lithopolis, there are a whole lot of apple orchards. It is so beautiful in the winter, with that blanket of snow laying at the base of those beautiful apple trees—but they're stark. There are no leaves. There are no apples.

Oh, but how it would get my attention if, driving through the row after row of those apple trees in January, with a blanket of white snow on the ground, I saw one of those apple trees hanging full of red, juicy, delicious apples. Apple trees do not have apples on them in the middle of January because the elements encircling them—the cold, the wind and the snow—will not allow them to bear fruit. So it is with human existence

When it's winter in your life, and it's impossible for you to bear fruit, God says, "I will cause you to bear fruit in the middle of the winter." And, the Book of Hebrews says, "By him therefore let us offer the sacrifice of praise to God continually, that is, the fruit of our lips giving thanks to his name" (13:15).

Do you know what God is saying? If you're walking through the winter of your life and you take His Word, mix it with faith in the generator of your spirit, and begin to praise Him, your words will become fruit. He will see the fruit of your lips, and in response perform that which you are asking of Him.

In other words, for those who will bear fruit in the middle of the winter, spring is on the horizon. For those who will act like they have victory, then victory is assured. For those who are weak, strength will invade their bodies. For those who will walk into the fiery furnace, the crackling flames will be commanded not to kindle upon them, For those who will walk into the water, it shall not overflow them. For those who have faith in God's faithfulness, and begin to declare unto Him the works of His hands, it will bear fruit in the middle of the winter.

Just as, according to the Hebrew writer, great men and women of the faith of bygone generations were chained to the walls and nailed to crosses for the cause of Christ . . . as they trusted God to deliver, so you can trust Him when you speak His Word. He will hasten His Word and perform it.

Like Paul, you may feel as if you are chained to the sewer systems of Rome, but if you can still speak, you will have a song to sing at midnight. They may put you in a hospital bed and tell you cancer is going to take your life. But, if you can still confess the Word, you can live and not die. Someone may tell you that your children aren't going to serve God, and there may be evidence to that fact, but you can begin to declare the decree of the Lord

Though you may suffer trouble, even as an evildoer, the Word of God inside you is not bound. And the Word that is within you shall spring up out of you.

The reason the devil tries to shut you up is because of God's Word. He knows the power of life and death are in your tongue. Your words are life to your spirit, body and soul and they are death to your adversary. Deuteronomy 27:8 declares, "And thou shalt offer peace offerings, and shalt eat there, and rejoice before the Lord thy God."

Delegated Authority

You and I are in authority on this earth. We have delegated authority. According to Isaiah 55, God sent His Word but it does not return to Him. Why? It is God's responsibility to send it but it is our responsibility to return it back to Him.

It is as though God makes a deposit of His Word in you, the same as you make a deposit in a bank. If I make a deposit in your bank account of $10,000, you will never drive the car that $10,000 could buy unless you learn how to make a withdrawal.

The Lord of Hosts makes the deposit of His Word and expects you to make the withdrawal because your faith will never rise above your confession. You are what you say because out of the abundance of the heart, the mouth speaks, and God establishes your word. But God said, If you will release that word back, it will accomplish that for which I sent it.

God sends His Word, "With His stripes you are healed" (1 Peter 2:24). It hits your spirit, and then you meditate on it.

Psalm 1:1-3 says, "Blessed is the man that walketh

not in the counsel of the ungodly, nor standeth in the way of sinners, nor sitteth in the seat of the scornful. But his delight is in the law of the Lord; and in his law doth he meditate day and night.

"And he shall be like a tree planted by the rivers of water, that bringeth forth his fruit in his season; his leaf also shall not wither; and whatsoever he doeth shall prosper."

Anybody can sing a tune on a clear day at noon. You and I need a song to sing at midnight. The season is winter, but we shall bring forth the fruit of our lips giving thanks unto His name. Our leaves shall not wither, and whatsoever we set our hands to shall prosper.

I remember a time in my early years of preaching that I had to put a voice to my faith and use my delegated authority in a particular situation.

I was scheduled to preach at another church when my vocal chords became swollen and began to bleed. At that time in my ministry I preached three Sunday services, a midweek service and several times on the road.

This night I was in terrible pain. When I arrived in town I was unable to speak. But in my hotel room I opened my Bible, walked around the room and began pointing to it. I didn't do this for an hour or two, but did it continuously, all day long. I would mouth the words, "I believe I receive when I pray. I thank you, Lord, my vocal chords are strong. I will preach tonight like a man from another world."

I walked around the room mouthing the Word of God but there was no sound. I would say things like:

But he was wounded for our transgressions, he was bruised for our iniquities: the chastisement of our peace was upon him; and with his stripes we are healed (Isaiah 53:5).

Bless the Lord, O my soul, and forget not all his benefits: Who forgiveth all thine iniquities; who healeth all thy diseases; Who redeemeth thy life from destruction; who crowneth thee with lovingkindness and tender mercies; Who satisfieth thy mouth with good things; so that thy youth is renewed like the eagle's (Psalm 103:2-5).

When I arrived at the service that night, I went through the entire praise and worship service singing, but not a note came out. But then something happened. When I walked to the pulpit, the first thing I did was grab the microphone, opened up my mouth and said, "Praise the Lord, everybody." My voice was strong and I preached until the people could hardly sit.

Hebrews 10:23 says, "Let us hold fast the profession of our faith without wavering; (for he is faithful that promised)."

Right now you can make a decision! You can allow your mountain to move your faith, or you can allow your faith to move your mountain. The choice is yours.

I have found out, if I believe in my heart and confess with my mouth, I can have whatsoever I say. Therefore when you pray, believe and you will receive.

Faith is not hard. You exercise faith every time you pray. You either believe you receive when you pray, or you believe you don't. You just have to turn the switch of faith on in order to receive your three-fold harvest.

When the expectation of your future
eclipses the pain of your past,
you are ready to give birth again.

Five

Faith's Delivery Room

"Abraham! Why do you want a son? You and your wife are well past the years to give birth! Maybe it would be best for you to just be happy with all of your houses, wealth and land."

"Jesse! You already have seven boys! Why do you want another one? You're getting old anyway!"

"Hannah! Why do you cry out like a drunken woman?" the high priest cried. "Am I not better to thee than ten sons?" her husband reasoned.

Each of these great men and women of God were scorned at, scoffed at and sneered at for their desire to have a child . . . but each of them had a promised seed:

Isaac was to be the promised offspring to Abraham, the father of many nations.

David was to encounter the Philistine giant and become the greatest king Israel would ever know.

Samuel was to become one of the greatest high priests of his day and lead God's people to repentance and holiness.

Like the seed of a man entering into a woman's body, something must happen from the point the Word comes in, until the point that your miracle manifests. Your spirit man, or your womb, is a generator. God's Word is a seed and it is very potent. In fact it is omnipotent, like God—it impregnates any womb it touches.

You cannot be around the Word of God and not become pregnant with joy, victory, money or whatever you need. It is not a hit or miss proposition, because the seed of the Word will burst through any obstacle. You have been marked for your three-fold miracle harvest since before you were ever born.

Jeremiah 1:5 states, "Before I formed thee in the belly I knew thee; and before thou camest forth out of the womb I sanctified thee, and I ordained thee a prophet unto the nations."

You are the seed who made it against all odds. Jeremiah 29:11 says, "For I know the thoughts that I think toward you, saith the Lord, thoughts of peace, and not of evil, to give you an expected end."

Birthing Your Miracle Harvest

In order to give birth to your three-fold miracle harvest, you have to go through a process much like what an expectant mother goes through in preparation for the birth of her child.

First, you have to have a sanctified womb. When a woman is pregnant her appetite begins to change. For the health of her small infant child she begins to eat differently. So it is with your spiritual womb. You cannot mix the seed of the Word of God with anything else. God will not be mixed with Baal, Molech or any other god. Your miracle harvest cannot be mixed with doubt and unbelief or you risk aborting your breakthrough. You must receive God's Word and then release it.

Mary, the mother of Jesus, believed and received the Word of the Lord in her spirit, for the Gospel of Luke records,

> And in the sixth month the angel of Gabriel was sent from God unto a city of Galilee, named Nazareth, to a virgin espoused to a man whose name was Joseph, of the house of David; and the virgin's name was Mary.
>
> And the angel came in unto her, and said, Hail, thou that art highly favoured, the Lord is with thee: blessed art thou among women. And when she saw him, she was troubled at his saying, and cast in her heart what manner of salutation this should be.
>
> And the angel said unto her, Fear not, Mary: for thou hast found favor with God. And, behold, thou shalt conceive in thy womb, and bring forth a son, and shalt call his name Jesus. He shall be great, and shall be called the Son of the Highest: and the Lord God shall give unto him the throne of his father David: And he shall reign over the house of Jacob for ever; and of his kingdom there shall be no end.

Then said Mary unto the angel, How shall this be, seeing I know not a man? And the angel answered and said unto her, The Holy Ghost shall come upon thee, and the power of the Highest shall overshadow thee: therefore also that holy thing which shall be born of thee shall be called the Son of God.

And, behold, thy cousin Elisabeth, she hath also conceived a son in her old age; and this is the sixth month with her, who was called barren. For with God nothing shall be impossible.

And Mary said, Behold the handmaid of the Lord; be it unto me according to thy word. And the angel departed from her (1:26-38).

Second you have to become pregnant. You have to make a commitment. It is at this point that you begin to watch your spiritual intake, because whatever goes into you affects your three-fold harvest outcome. Mark paints a very graphic description of the potential hazards to the seed sown in your life when it says:

And he taught them many things by parables, and said unto them in his doctrine, Hearken; Behold, there went out a sower to sow:

And it came to pass, as he sowed, some fell by the way side, and the fowls of the air came and devoured it up. And some fell on stony ground, where it had not much earth; and immediately it sprang up, because it had no depth of earth:

But when the sun was up, it was scorched; and because it had no root, it withered away. And some fell among thorns, and the thorns grew up, and choked it, and it yielded no fruit.

And other fell on good ground, and did yield fruit that sprang up and increased; and brought forth, some thirty, and some sixty, and some an hundred (4:2-8).

Third, the signs of birth begin to start with labor pains. When a woman is in labor, she may not like to shout, but she doesn't necessarily have a choice in the matter because the pain is setting in. Her hair is down, her perfume sweated off and the signs of birthing new life are near.

It is a proven fact that labor of giving birth is one of the closest experiences to death. It may feel like you're going to die, but hold on—life is just around the corner!

Fourth, when you begin to experience spiritual labor pains is when the delivery of your miracle manifests. Here you have the prayer of faith that refuses to take no for an answer. But most importantly, you have the prayer of agreement. You have agreement with God and agreement with someone else.

Just as a baby is rarely born when you expect it to be,

so it is with your miracle. It comes at the most inconvenient time, just so God can let you know it didn't have anything to do with you. It may seem like you have been through a bloody battle, but your victory has been sealed.

Next, when that child is born, the joy of seeing this beautiful miracle outweighs all of the pain of labor. That's the way it is when your harvest comes. Remember, "All things are possible to him that believeth" (Mark 9:23).

Hold on my child. "Weeping may endure for a night, but joy cometh in the morning" (Psalm 30:5).

"Cast not away therefore your confidence, which hath great recompence of reward" (Hebrews 10:35).

"And let us not be weary in well doing: for in due season we shall reap, if we faint not" (Galatians 6:9).

Your Release Valve

You are the living ark of God. There is resurrection power inside of you. John 7:38 records these words, "He that believeth on me, as the scripture hath said, out of his belly shall flow rivers of living water."

It is from this passage of Scripture that we derive the concept of a generator. You see, a generator receives one kind of energy, and it has the ability to transform it into another form of energy.

Generators operate by pouring gasoline into them. Once this is done, any piece of equipment that runs on electricity can be plugged into it and it will run perfectly.

Your spirit is a womb, and it receives energy from the

seed of the Word of God, like a generator receives gasoline. When you put Scripture after Scripture in your spirit, out of you comes another form of energy, or power. From the depths of your spirit comes mountain moving power.

You are a creative force in the world. We've studied throughout this book that faith and the spoken word can shape your today and your tomorrow because Hebrews 11:3 says, "Through faith we understand that the worlds were framed by the Word of God, so that things which are seen were not made of things which do appear." Faith is the tangibility of things you cannot see or perceive with your senses. In this final hour you and I must learn to access the spirit realm and reap our three-fold harvest: spiritually, physically and financially.

Give Birth Again

In order to keep reproducing a continuous flood of miracle harvests the final thing you must remember is that when the promise in front of you gets bigger than the pain behind you, you're ready to give birth again. When you begin to walk in this revelation you will be producing miracles faster than the devil can try to stop you. Exodus chapter 1 records these words:

> And the children of Israel were fruitful, and increased abundantly, and multiplied, and waxed exceeding mighty; and the land was filled with them. Now there arose up a new king over Egypt, which knew not Joseph.

And he said unto his people, Behold, the people of the children of Israel are more and mightier than we: Come on, let us deal wisely with them; lest they multiply, and it come to pass, that, when there falleth out any war, they join also unto our enemies, and fight against us, and so get them up out of the land.

Therefore they did set over them taskmasters to afflict them with their burdens. And they built for Pharaoh treasure cities, Pithom and Raamses. But the more they afflicted them, the more they multiplied and grew. And they were grieved because of the children of Israel.

And the king of Egypt spake to the Hebrew midwives, of which the name of the one was Shiphrah, and the name of the other Puah: And he said, When ye do the office of a midwife to the Hebrew women, and see them upon the stools; if it be a son, then ye shall kill him: but if it be a daughter, then she shall live.

But the midwives feared God, and did not as the king of Egypt commanded them, but saved the men children alive. And the king of Egypt called for the midwives, and said unto them, Why have ye done this thing, and have saved the men children alive?

And the midwives said unto Pharaoh, Because the Hebrew women are not as the Egyptian women; for they are lively, and are delivered ere the midwives come in unto them. Therefore God dealt well with the midwives: and the people multiplied, and waxed very mighty (1:7-12, 15-20).

This is the year of harvest. You will be overcome with the blessings of the Lord. What God has promised, the devil cannot steal. John 10:10 says, "The thief cometh not, but for to steal, and to kill, and to destroy: I am come that they might have life, and that they might have it more abundantly."

God wants to reproduce life inside of your spiritual womb. He wants to make that dream which was dead and barren come to life again. He wants to impart unto you a spirit of reproduction, spiritually, to deliver captive souls out of the clutches of Satan.

He wants you to conceive your physical harvest with a word, "He sent his word, and healed them, and delivered them from their destructions."

He wants to impregnate you with a financial promise, "But my God shall supply all your need according to his riches in glory by Christ Jesus" (Philippians 4:19).

Push Until Something Happens
Maybe you think your destiny has already passed you by. Possibly you think you have already missed your opportunity. Perhaps you have been thinking, "Surely, God isn't ever going to do anything with me again."

Remember Jesus as He hung upon an old rugged

cross. The ringing of the hammer was heard, and nails parted sinew and flesh. They wrapped Him in grave clothes and laid Him in a borrowed tomb, but there was a word just waiting.

For thou wilt not leave my soul in hell; neither wilt thou suffer thine Holy One to see corruption (Psalm 16:10).

That word couldn't manifest in Nazareth, nor in Bethlehem. Its time had not come. It was not birthing season.

The words of the Psalmist waited through Elijah, Elisha, Ezekiel, Daniel and 400 years of silence.

Let me just interject this thought: When it seems the Lord is being quiet in your circumstance, just remember He is up to something.

Sometimes you feel like you can't give birth to your miracle. You just can't get it out, but somehow, when you start to see the head of your miracle crowning, and the doctor begins to yell, "It's coming!" Don't give up—push a little harder. Push until something begins to happen!

In the spirit realm, throughout the earth, there is a stirring. It's birthing time.

Somewhere in the eternal realm of glory there is a word, a promise, floating around for you. It is just about to touch your sanctified womb. You are about to conceive again. God has a destiny for you. The harvest of your promise has come so powerfully as to defeat all of the alien forces of the Antichrist. Victory is on the way.

Let them throw Paul and Silas in the Roman jail. Their God is able. Throw Daniel in the lion's den. He'll turn his face toward Jerusalem, offer his prayer to God, pillow his head in the shaggy mane of the lion and sleep like a baby all night long, for his God is able.

Ephesians 3:20 says, "Now unto him that is able to do exceeding abundantly above all that we ask or think, according to the power that worketh in us."

God is not only just able, but also He is able to do exceedingly, abundantly above all you can ask or think! Take special notice of this: that it's **according to His power!** That takes the pressure off because it's His power we're dependent upon and not our own!

The heartbeat of God is that none should perish,
but that all come to the knowledge of the truth.

Six

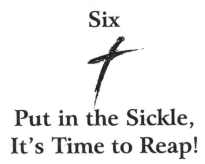

Put in the Sickle, It's Time to Reap!

We are living in the final hour of human history. Time as we know it is collapsing all around us, and we have the Spirit of God within us to reap our three-fold harvest spiritually, physically and financially.

A Harvest of Souls

This final generation is about to experience the greatest harvest the world has ever seen. Revelation 21 declares that nations will be born in a day.

The heartbeat of God is that none would perish but that all come to the knowledge of the truth. What is His vision? John 3:16 and 17 says it best, "For God so loved the world, that he gave his only begotten Son, that whosoever believeth in him should not perish, but have everlasting life. For God sent not his Son into the world to condemn the world; but that the world through him might be saved."

The Lord wants a great harvest of souls and He will go to any length to get them. Matthew 22:1-10 says:

And Jesus answered and spake unto them again by parables, and said, The kingdom of heaven is like unto a certain king, which made a marriage for his son, and sent forth his servants to call them that were bidden to the wedding: and they would not come.

Again, he sent forth other servants, saying, Tell them which are bidden, Behold, I have prepared my dinner: my oxen and my fatlings are killed, and all things are ready: come unto the marriage.

But they made light of it, and went their ways, one to his farm, another to his merchandise: And the remnant took his servants, and entreated them spitefully, and slew them.

But when the king heard thereof, he was wroth: and he sent forth his armies, and destroyed those murderers, and burned up their city. Then saith he to his servants, The wedding is ready, but they which were bidden were not worthy.

Go ye therefore into the highways, and as many as ye shall find, bid to the marriage. So those servants went out into the highways, and gathered together all as many as they found, both bad and good: and the wedding was furnished with guests.

The final chapter has already been written and we

come out on the winning side. Just like the wedding feast, there will be more souls saved from every kindred, creed, country and kingdom than those whom the enemy has deceived.

"His lord answered and said unto him, Thou wicked and slothful servant, thou knewest that I reap where I sowed not, and gather where I have not strawed" (Matthew 25:26).

Isaiah 2:2,3 proclaims, "And it shall come to pass in the last days, that the mountain of the LORD's house shall be established in the top of the mountains, and shall be exalted above the hills; and all nations shall flow unto it.

"And many people shall go and say, Come ye, and let us go up to the mountain of the Lord, to the house of the God of Jacob; and he will teach us of his ways, and we will walk in his paths: for out of Zion shall go forth the law, and the word of the Lord from Jerusalem."

The time has come to enlist in this revolutionary army, follow our orders, take up our arms, invade the corridors of the doomed and the damned, engage our arch-enemy, Satan, and set this hell-bound generation free.

The eyes of the Lord are running to and fro for a remnant who will stand in the gap and make up the hedge for humanity. He is looking for some warriors who don't have to be right, recognized or rewarded. For these alone will reap the end time harvest of souls, receive His eternal reward and righteous commendation.

A Harvest of Healing
Did you know that there are only three questions

people have in regard to their healing? The first question is *"Will God heal me?"* The answer to this question is found in the story of Luke chapter 5:13. Jesus proclaimed, "I will: be thou clean!"

The second question is *"Can God heal me?"* This question is answered in Mark 9 when one of the scribes took his son who had been afflicted with a dumb spirit to Jesus' disciples and they could do nothing. He then took the child to Jesus and said unto Him, "If you canst do any thing, have compassion on us and help us." Jesus responded to them, "If thou canst believe, all things are possible to him that believeth."

The third and most important question is, *"Will I be healed?"* This was the question posed to the man at the pool of Bethesda, in John 5:6 as he waited for just the right time to enter the pool, at the stirring of the waters by the angel. But Jesus confronted the man by asking him this startling question, "Wilt thou be made whole?"

May I remind you that the Bible declares, Today is the day of salvation and now is the appointed time (2 Corinthians 6:2). Salvation means healing, deliverance, financial prosperity—whatever you need!

As the curtain rises on the last act of this human drama, no longer will we have to be in bondage to sickness, disease and infirmity. Like the man with the withered hand, we will stretch forth our pain and be made whole (Mark 3).

We won't have to live in constant agony because there is a restoration of healing coming to the body of Christ. There will not be one sick among us according to Psalm

105:37, "He brought them forth also with silver and gold: and there was not one feeble person among their tribes."

If you need the healing touch of Jesus to enter into your life, Mark 6:56 says, "And whithersoever He entered, into villages, or cities, or country, they laid the sick in the streets, and besought him that they might touch if it were but the border of his garment: and as many as touched him were made whole."

Jesus is moved with compassion by your greatest burden and your greatest yoke of bondage. Maybe that burden is the healing you so desperately need. Maybe it is AIDS that has attacked your body or migraine headaches or the loneliness of divorce. Nothing is too insignificant to Him.

Satan may have plotted his most diabolical plan to keep you from receiving your miracle. But 1 John chapter 5 and verse 18 says, "But he that is begotten of God keepeth himself, and that wicked one toucheth him not."

Jesus is not only the physician of your body, He is the physician of your mind and your spirit. He has the cure, through the Cross of Calvary, to cleanse you of whatever ails you. He wants to take control of your situation. He wants to touch you where others refused or have failed to do so.

A Financial Harvest

God wants you to break free from the slave mentality and to receive your financial harvest. He desires to bless you. He has already scheduled your harvest in every area

75

of your life . . . your health . . . your body . . . your family . . . your finances.

Luke chapter 4 verses 18 and 19 say:

"The Spirit of the Lord [is] upon me, because he has anointed me [the anointed one, the messiah] to preach the good news (the Gospel) to the poor; he has sent me to announce release to the captives and recovery of sight to the blind, to send forth as delivered those who are oppressed [who are downtrodden, bruised, crushed, and broken down by calamity], to **proclaim** the accepted and acceptable year of the Lord" (Amplified).

I like to say it this way, "The day when salvation and the free favors of God profusely abound!"

You are <u>anointed</u>, my Bible says, which means painted with the scent of God's fragrance to attract the blessing and the favor of God!

But let me share this with you: the greatest satanic opposition always comes right before your greatest breakthrough!

The Bible says, "He that observeth the wind shall not sow; and he that regardeth the clouds shall not reap" (Ecclesiastes 11:4).

Right now, I want you to draw a line in the spiritual sand and step across it and proclaim, "Today, I enter the promised land. Today, the promise is mine. Today, I have more than enough!"

I refuse to ever be comfortable with lack again: lack of resources, lack of health and lack of freedom in my spirit.

This revolution is not for the timid or weak, but the strong and brave who have stepped over the line and out of the comfort zone. It is for those who have decided to become disciples of Christ.

Sound the alarm! A Holy Ghost invasion is taking place! Man your battle stations, ready your weapons and lock and load. Let the revolution begin with a shout for Him who hath called us to war and empowered us to win!

Thrust in thy sickle, and reap:
for the time is come for thee to reap;
for the harvest of the earth is ripe (Revelation 14:15).

Epilogue

✝

Your Harvest is Come!

Hosea, Amos and Zechariah all prophesied Jesus would come. Malachi said it this way, "Behold, I will send my messenger, and he shall prepare the way before me: and the Lord, whom ye seek, shall suddenly come to his temple, even the messenger of the covenant, whom ye delight in: behold, he shall come, saith the Lord of hosts" (3:1).

In the town of Mobile Bay, Alabama there is a unusual occurrence that happens once or twice a year. It's infamously known as "Jubilee."

Jubilee occurs when there is a shift in the chemistry which suddenly causes all types of marine life to be washed to shore. When this transpires someone will cry out ecstatically, "Jubilee"!

Suddenly, this quiet town turns into chaos as people from dentists to druggists, shopkeepers to street sweepers begin to grab anything they can find in order to reap a great harvest of fish.

One of the interesting facts about Jubilee is that when they pull in their catch not only do they harvest the good fish, but also they harvest the bad fish as well. (Morning Star Publications, 1997).

The harvest we are going to reap is a wonderful

79

illustration of what is taking place today. Jesus is shouting, "Jubilee"! We must say, "Amen!" and declare it to be so!

We have prayed long enough for our children to return to God. We have fasted long enough for deliverance in our minds. We have believed long enough for that infirmity to leave our bodies.

The place is here, the time is now. We are about to give birth to a miracle.

There is a birthing about to take place. Isaiah 60:1, 2 says, "Arise, shine; for thy light is come, and the glory of the Lord is risen upon thee. For, behold, the darkness shall cover the earth, and gross darkness the people: but the Lord shall arise upon thee, and his glory shall be seen upon thee."

We will be a people who God has sovereignly declared us to be. We will accomplish that which He has placed in front of us to do.

There is a three-fold birthing coming: a birthing in the spiritual, a birthing in the physical and a birthing in the financial areas of your life. The Ancient of Days is about to impregnate this final generation just one more time with His Word in order that we may reap where we did not sow.

Throughout the ages, countries and kingdoms have been birthed on the battlefield of a revolutionary movement. God is about to give birth to the greatest revolutionary movement that the world has ever known.

Are you ready?

Power concedes nothing without a demand. Freedom is never granted voluntarily by the oppressor. It must be demanded by the oppressed.

It's time to enlist in this army. It's time to take up the sword of the Spirit which is the Word of God. It's time to stop hiding out in the devil's demilitarized zone.

It's time to "thrust in thy sickle, and reap: for the time is come for thee to reap; for the harvest of the earth is ripe" (Revelation 14:15).

How long until you reap your three-fold miracle harvest? Not long! Just around the corner, in a moment, sooner than you think . . . *your harvest is come!*

Scriptural Keys to Birthing Your Miracle Harvest

"I have been young, and now am old; yet have I not seen the righteous forsaken, nor his seed begging bread" (Psalm 37:25)

"Death and life are in the power of the tongue: and they that love it shall eat the fruit thereof" (Proverb 18:21).

"Money answereth all things" (Ecclesiastes 10:19).

"For as the rain cometh down, and the snow from heaven, and returneth not thither, but watereth the earth, and maketh it bring forth and bud, that it may give seed to the sower, and bread to the eater: so shall my word be that goeth forth out of my mouth: it shall not return unto me void, but it shall accomplish that which I please, and it shall prosper in the thing whereto I sent it" (Isaiah 55:10).

"The Spirit of the Lord God is upon me; because the Lord hath anointed me to preach good tidings unto the meek; he hath sent me to bind up the brokenhearted, to proclaim liberty to the captives, and the opening of the prison to them that are bound;

"To proclaim the acceptable year of the Lord, and the day of vengeance of our God; to comfort all that mourn; to appoint unto them that mourn in Zion, to give unto them beauty for ashes, the oil of joy for mourning, the garment of praise for the spirit of heaviness; that they might be called trees of righteousness, the planting of the Lord, that he might be glorified" (Isaiah 61:1-3).

"Moreover the word of the Lord came unto me, saying, Jeremiah, what seest thou? And I said, I see a rod of an almond tree. Then said the Lord unto me, thou hast well seen: for I will hasten my word to perform it" (Jeremiah 1:11, 12).

"For I know the thoughts that I think toward you, saith the Lord, thoughts of peace, and not of evil, to give you an expected end" (Jeremiah 29:11).

"My people are destroyed for lack of knowledge: because thou hast rejected knowledge, I will also reject thee, that thou shalt be no priest to me: seeing thou hast forgotten the law of thy God, I will also forget thy children" (Hosea 4:6).

"Be glad then, ye children of Zion, and rejoice in the Lord your God: for he hath given you the former rain moderately, and he will cause to come down for you the rain, the former rain, and the latter rain in the first month. And the floors shall be full of wheat, and the fats shall overflow with wine and oil. And I will restore to you the years that the locust hath eaten, the cankerworm, and the caterpillar, and the palmerworm, my great army which I sent among you" (Joel 2:23-25).

"Behold, the days come, saith the Lord, that the plowman shall overtake the reaper, and the treader of grapes him that soweth seed; and the mountains shall drop sweet wine, and all the hills shall melt" (Amos 9:13).

"Bring ye all the tithes into the storehouse, that there may be meat in mine house, and prove me now herewith, saith the Lord of hosts, if I will not open you the windows of heaven, and pour you out a blessing, that there shall not be room enough to receive it" (Malachi 3:10).

"And he said, So is the kingdom of God, as if a man should cast seed into the ground; And should sleep, and rise night and day, and the seed should spring and grow up, he knoweth not how. For the earth bringeth forth fruit of herself; first the blade, then the ear, after that the full corn in the ear. But when the fruit is brought forth, immediately he putteth in the sickle, because the harvest is come" (Mark 4:26-29).

"Jesus said unto him, If thou canst believe, all things are possible to him that believeth" (Mark 9:23).

"And Jesus answering saith unto them, have faith in God. For verily I say unto you, that whosoever shall say unto this mountain, be thou removed, and be thou cast into the sea; and shall not doubt in his heart, but shall believe that those things which he saith shall come to pass; he shall have whatsoever he saith. Therefore I say unto you, what things soever ye desire, when ye pray, believe that ye receive them, and ye shall have them" (Mark 11:22-24).

"Say not ye, there are yet four months, and then cometh harvest? Behold, I say unto you, lift up your eyes, and look on the fields; for they are white already to harvest"(John 4:35).

"He that believeth on me, as the scripture hath said, out of his belly shall flow rivers of living water" (John 7:38).

"Repent ye therefore, and be converted, that your sins may be blotted out, when the times of refreshing shall come from the presence of the Lord; And he shall send Jesus Christ, which before was preached unto you: whom the heaven must receive until the times of restitution of all things, which God hath spoken by the mouth of all his holy prophets since the world began" (Acts 3:19-21).

"We having the same spirit of faith, according as it is written, I believed, and therefore have I spoken; we also believe, and therefore speak" (2 Corinthians 4:13).

"For we walk by faith, not by sight" (2 Corinthians 5:7).

"God can pour on the blessings in astonishing ways so that you're ready for anything and everything, more than just ready to do what needs to be done. As one psalmist puts it, "He throws caution to the winds, giving to the needy in reckless abandon. His right-living, right-giving ways never run out, never wear out" (2 Corinthians 9:8,9 The Message Bible).

"Be careful for nothing; but in every thing by prayer and supplication with thanksgiving let your requests be made known unto God" (Philippians 4:6).

"Now faith is the substance of things hoped for, the evidence of things not seen" (Hebrews 11:1).

"But without faith it is impossible to please him: for he that cometh to God must believe that he is, and that he is a rewarder of them that diligently seek him" (Hebrews 11:6).

"Go to now, ye rich men, weep and howl for your miseries that shall come upon you. Your riches are corrupted, and your garments are motheaten. Your gold and silver is cankered; and the rust of them shall be a witness against you, and shall eat your flesh as it were fire. Ye have heaped treasure together for the last days" (James 5:1-3).

"And this is the confidence that we have in him, that, if we ask any thing according to his will, he heareth us: and if we know that he hear us, whatsoever we ask, we know that we have the petitions that we desired of him. (1 John 5:14,15)

"And another angel came out of the temple, crying with a loud voice to him that sat on the cloud, thrust in thy sickle, and reap: for the time is come for thee to reap; for the harvest of the earth is ripe" (Revelation 14:15).

ABOUT THE AUTHOR

Rod Parsley began his ministry as an energetic 19-year-old in the backyard of his parents' Ohio home. The fresh, "old-time Gospel" approach of Parsley's delivery immediately attracted a hungry, God-seeking audience. From the 17 people who attended Parsley's first 1977 backyard meeting, the crowds rapidly grew.

Today, as the pastor of Columbus, Ohio's 5,200-seat World Harvest Church, Parsley oversees World Harvest Christian Academy, World Harvest Bible College, Bridge of Hope missions and outreach, and "Breakthrough," World Harvest Church's daily and weekly television broadcast. Parsley's message to "Repair the Breach, Raise the Standard and Reap the Harvest" not only extends across North America, but also spans the globe to nearly 136 nations via television and shortwave radio.

Thousands in arenas across the country and around the world experience the saving, healing and delivering message of Jesus Christ as Parsley calls people back to Bible basics.

Rod Parsley currently resides in Pickerington, Ohio, with his wife, Joni, and their two children, Ashton and Austin.

OTHER BOOKS BY
ROD PARSLEY

Backside of Calvary
Breakthrough Quotes
Ten Golden Keys Special Edition Bridge Builders' Bible
The Commanded Blessing
Covenant Blessings
Daily Breakthrough
The Day Before Eternity
Free at Last
God's Answer to Insufficient Funds
He Sent His Word and Healed Them
Holiness: Living Leaven Free
I'm Glad You Asked
The Jubilee Anointing
My Promise Is the Palace
No Dry Season (best seller)
No More Crumbs (best seller)
Power Through the Baptism of the Holy Ghost
Renamed and Redeemed
Repairers of the Breach
Serious Survival Strategies
Ten Golden Keys to Your Abundance
Tribulation to Triumph

For information about *Breakthrough*,
World Harvest Church or to receive a product list of the
many books and audio and video tapes
by Rod Parsley write or call:

Breakthrough
P.O. Box 32932
Columbus, Ohio 43232-0932
(614) 837-1990

For information about World Harvest Bible College,
write or call:

World Harvest Bible College
P.O. Box 32901
Columbus, Ohio 43232-0901
(614) 837-4088

If you need prayer, the *Breakthrough* prayer line is open
24 hours a day, 7 days a week.
(614) 837-3232

Visit Rod Parsley at his website address:
www.breakthrough.net

Notes

<u>Notes</u>

<u>Notes</u>

<u>Notes</u>

<u>Notes</u>

<u>Notes</u>

<u>Notes</u>

<u>Notes</u>

<u>Notes</u>

Notes

<u>Notes</u>

<u>Notes</u>

Notes